Children
Eyes of the Soul

To Linda

With warmest wishes -

Margaret Woodson Nea

Published in the United States of America
Printed by Mobility Printing, Richmond, Virginia
Designed by Melissa J. Savage, Richmond, Virginia

For inquiries about additional copies of this book, an exhibit of photographs, or to purchase prints write to:
Margaret Woodson Nea, Post Office Box 1156, White Stone, Virginia 22578.

With gratitude — to Kitty for her spirit of generosity, to Jim for his inspiration and sense of beauty, to Ben for his vision in making these books possible,
        to Beth for her patience and artist's eye, to Freeman for his guidance in teaching me to see with new eyes

For my grandchildren

Mary

Clay

Katie

Ellie

Jack

Let there be peace on earth and let it begin with me.

Jill Jackson and Sy Miller

Introduction

In the fading light of the afternoon sun, the interior of the temple is enveloped in almost total darkness. At the doorway, I watch Siriarpra and her grandmother, Malai, take off their shoes to enter a holy place. Reverently, they walk inside. A single shaft of light highlights a small portion of the teak floor. All the other pilgrims and tourists have left the temple, and the three of us are alone. It is Siriarpra's first day away from her village home, her first time to be in a city, and her first occasion to enter the Ubon Ratchanthani Temple.

Malai, the grandmother, folds her hands facing the altar. With a graceful movement, holding her palms together and moving them up to her chin, she bends over, lowering her head deeply. Then she sits, kneels forward, and, bowing in prayer, she touches her head to the floor. Siriarpra follows Malai's lead. She also folds her hands and bows her tiny, five-year-old body to the floor. Seated near them, I leave my camera in my lap, not wanting to intrude on the intimacy of their sacred time together.

After a time, Malai returns to a sitting position to meditate. Siriarpra again watches her grandmother. She sits close beside her.

Soon it is apparent that Siriarpra is anxious to move. She gently stands. Tentatively she begins to move first one foot and then the other. As I watch her sense of wonder, I am curious about the floor in her own home. Is it the usual dirt floor of a Thai village hut? Is this the first time her feet, in her little white socks, have ever touched a polished, wooden floor?

Feeling the wood's smoothness, Siriarpra's feet glide gracefully. Her hands, beautifully coordinated, move from side to side next to her face in the ceremonial gestures of the Thai traditional dance.

Malai looks at Siriarpra, and I know from the concerned expression on her face that she is weighing what she must do as a grandmother. She reaches out to touch Siriarpra and then hesitates. Should she stop her granddaughter, reminding her that she is in a sacred place? I watch, wondering what she will do.

I see Malai's expression relax. I can tell she understands that the mystery of the sacred is moving in her granddaughter. She allows Siriarpra to continue. As if caught by an inner spirit, Siriarpra has entered her own world, hearing her own music. The dance takes over. Her body is visible poetry in motion. Now, through the lens of my camera, my eyes follow her. Through the lens of my heart, my soul takes joy in her unrestrained grace.

Against the background of silence, Siriarpra is flowing, filled with her own rhythm and energy and spontaneous delight. Her small body is the outward expression of her inner world. Her spirit is free and expressive, emerging, awakening, gliding, dancing, whirling.

Photographing as quickly as I can in this darkened space, I am transfixed by Siriarpra, who fills the stillness with her own ecstasy. She dances intuitively, naturally, with her whole being, bending over, reaching upward, in touch with divine mystery. I am witness to a holy moment.

All of us wish that every child could have similar moments of delight as found in Siriarpra's graceful dance. Evoking beauty born of her spirit, her dance exemplifies a child's way into pure joy. We also want children to have moments of sacred time shared with parents and grandparents. Siriarpra is my sponsored child in Thailand, yet she represents the universal child, the hundreds of children I have encountered photographing around the world.

Opportunities to photograph in Asia, Africa, and South America have broadened my vision in every sense of the word. Despite great distances, on my journey to some of the most remote places of the world, I find more similarities than differences. By crossing borders, I find common ground.

From the high Andes Mountains to the savannas of Africa, each journey speaks to my heart. I travel with organizations deeply committed to bringing hope to some of the darkest corners of the world. For the children I meet, life is hard, a constant struggle. They lack material possessions, live in dire circumstances, yet I continue to be amazed by their exuberance for life. Their infectious spirits transform me, and I see our world with new eyes.

I go with an open heart, with open arms, and open eyes, and the children open their hearts to me. With the universal language of a smile, we reach out to one another with a kinship that knows no borders. In village after village, the children come running from all directions with their shy smiles that inevitably turn into gales of laughter. I am a curiosity with my cameras around my neck. "Hujambo, hujambo," they cry out on the dusty plains in Kenya. Standing quietly beside the mountain paths in Nepal, I hear them calling, "Namas-te, namas-te," as they bow, "I honor you, I honor the god within you."

No matter the country, no matter their native word of greeting, the children are immensely welcoming. They invite me into their homes, made of bamboo, corrugated tin, or mud brick, and make me feel a part of their life, giving me blessings when I enter and blessings when I leave.

As they follow me around their village, I am privileged to see a part of their hearts, to participate in their enthusiasm and spontaneity. I am honored by their belief that all visitors are blessings. Their hospitality often includes songs, prayers, dances, and ceremonies. I come away enriched by their traditions and culture and generous spirits.

Living close to the natural world, to the rhythms of the earth, dependent on the cycles of the seasons, the children carry something of the eternal. They are ageless, timeless, with a nobility of spirit. It seems I have strayed into another era. I look at my photographs when I return to my home and think the images could have been taken centuries ago.

There is much to learn from these children. In contrast to our modern-day world, I learn from the simplicity of their everyday lives. I learn from their wisdom far beyond their years. I learn from their boundless energy, their lively spirits, their openness to grace. As I watch them hard at work, I learn from the sense of responsibility that they manifest at a young age. A young girl carries her brother on her back while their mother works in the fields. A turbaned boy herds sheep along a dirt road to new pastures. A child bends over to milk the family goat. A small girl kneads bread to bake for her family's one meal of the day. Laughing girls balance earthen pots filled with water on their heads to carry to their families. These children are my teachers. When the student is ready, the Buddhists say, the teacher will appear.

Through my photographs, I want the faces of the children to be seen, their stories imagined, their eyes to speak of their souls. Sometimes their eyes twinkle with joy. Other times their eyes tell of the sadness of their region. Always they make an enduring impression.

Jason Elliot has said, "Once snared...one never fully leaves: a portion of one's heart is forever woven into the fabric of that place." Certainly that is true for me. My heart is interwoven not only into the places I have traveled but also with the children I have met. Embedded in my soul are their lovely faces and haunting eyes, their quite dignity and infectious enthusiasm, their joyful laughter and poignant tears.

Children are a precious treasure to be loved, nurtured, and protected. This collection of images is a tribute to the courage of the children I have met in remote places around the world. It is a celebration of their resilience and endurance. It is an invitation to enter into their lives, both heart-rending and enriching. It is my way to honor these children whose grace-filled spirit enriches my life.

There is only one child in the world
And that child's name is All Children.

Carl Sandburg

It is only with the heart that one can see rightly ....

Antoine de St. Exupéry

Every soul is to be cherished ....

Every flower is to bloom.

Alice Walker

Children add to the wonder of being alive.

Herbert Hoover

Their souls dwell in the house of tomorrow.

Kahlil Gibran

We believe in the intrinsic worth of each child.

Christian Children's Fund

If we are to reach real peace in the world ... we shall have to begin with children.

Mahatma Gandhi

The most beautiful things in the world ... must be felt with the heart.

Helen Keller

Each birth is a glimpse into the mystery of creation.

Margaret Guenther

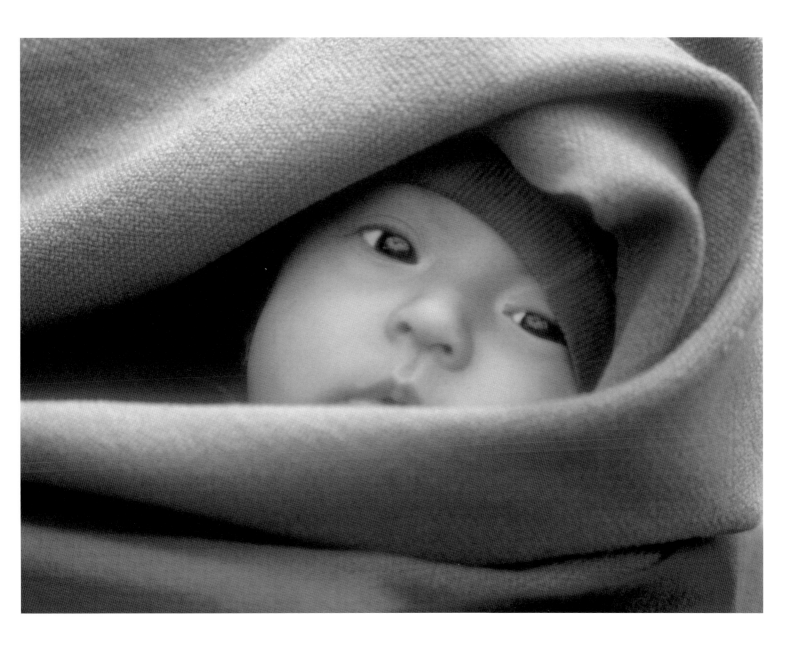

Adult and child share one world, and all generations are needed.

Pearl Buck

Let the little children come unto me, for of such is the kingdom of heaven.

Matthew 19:13-14

Every story is a luminous thread that becomes a part of a larger fabric ....

Sue Monk Kidd

Each individual is a marvelous opportunity.

The Dalai Lama

The privilege of a lifetime is being who you are.

Joseph Campbell

May the sun bring you new energy by day

May the moon softly restore you by night

May the rain wash away your worries

May the breeze blow new strength into your being

May you walk gently through the world and

know its beauty all the days of your life.

Apache Blessing

Nobody has ever measured how much the heart can hold.

Zelda Fitzgerald

Can you tell how it is ... that light comes into the soul?

Henry David Thoreau

It is the calm acceptance of everything that comes ...
that makes their presence so impressive.

Peter Matthiessen

In the beautiful gesture, Namas-te, we worship God in each person.

Bede Griffiths

Children carry a promise with them, a hidden treasure ...
to be led into the open through education.

Henri J. M. Nouwen

I wish peace without any violence.

I wish the poor always had food on their table.

Franciele
A Christian Children's Fund
Sponsored Child

We are all the same. We are not different from one another.
We all belong to one family.

N. Kosi Johnson

There is a self in each of us aching to be born.

Alan Jones

In the sweetness of friendship let there be laughter and the sharing of pleasure.

Kahlil Gibran

As we listen to her voice, we look deep into our own souls,

for it awakens sensations and feelings which we ... thought were lost forever.

Rigoberta Menchú

There are only two lasting bequests we can hope to give our children.
One of them is roots, the other, wings.

Hodding Carter

Where there is great love, there are always miracles.

Willa Cather

Our most common link is that we inhabit this small planet.
We all breathe the same air. We all cherish our children's children.

John Fitzgerald Kennedy

Blessed are the peace-makers; for they shall be called the children of God.

Matthew 5:9

In a baby's eyes, the wonder of creation shines, the miracle of new life.

Katherine Davis

Laughter is the closest thing to the grace of God.

Karl Barth

It is the child who is God's messenger of love and hope for the future.

Marian Wright Edelman

To him in whom love dwells, the whole world is but one family.

Buddhist Saying

Each person can make a difference ...

and together we can do those things that we cannot do separately.

Dr. John L. Peters

Lord, make us instruments of your peace.

Where there is hatred, let us sow love;

where there is injury, pardon;

where there is discord, union;

where there is doubt, faith;

where there is despair, hope;

where there is darkness, light;

where there is sadness, joy.

Grant that we may not so much seek to be consoled as to console;

to be understood as to understand;

to be loved as to love.

For it is in giving that we receive;

it is in pardoning that we are pardoned;

and it is in dying that we are born to eternal life.

Prayer of St. Francis

Visiting ... these (children), you immediately realize you have been given an astonishing gift and having received something so valuable, how could anyone not feel the urge to give something back?

Jon Krakauer

As a photographer, it is an enormous privilege to photograph children in some of the most remote areas of the world. I travel with organizations that care deeply for children. They are dedicated to improving the economic, social, and spiritual conditions where basic survival is imperiled. I find the organizations have many similarities. All emphasize the need to educate children and families. All seek ways to feed the hungry, to provide access to safe water, to protect against disease. All look for solutions to strengthen communities and encourage self-sustainability. All understand the need for caring for others by remembering the words, "Love one another."

As you look into the eyes of these children, please pray for them. As you look into your own heart, please consider giving generously.

Christian Children's Fund

Knowing that children are humanity's most valuable resource, Christian Children's Fund, since its inception in 1938, has created an environment of hope and respect for needy children of all cultures and beliefs in which they have opportunities to achieve their full potential. The majority of funding comes through monthly sponsorships to provide practical tools for positive change for children, their families, and communities. Christian Children's Fund assists more than ten million children in thirty-three countries, including the United States.

Christian Children's Fund, 2821 Emerywood Pky., Richmond, VA 23294
www.ChristianChildrensFund.org   1.800.776.6767

Bread for the World

Bread for the World seeks justice for the world's hungry people by advocating for legislation to fight hunger around the world and by engaging in research and education on policies related to hunger and development.

Bread for the World, 50 F St., Suite 500, Washington, D. C. 20001
www.bread.org   1.800.82.BREAD

World Neighbors

World Neighbors, was founded in 1951 by Dr. John Peters (1907-1992), twice nominated for a Nobel Peace Prize. Dr. Peters described World Neighbors as "an educational program with its curriculum being agriculture, literacy, public health, and village industries. Its campus is the farm (and) the mud hut." It works in partnership with the rural poor in hundreds of villages throughout Asia, Africa, and Latin America. By strengthening the capacity of individuals and communities, their programs empower people to solve their own problems related to hunger, disease, and poverty.

World Neighbors, 4127 NW 122 St., Oklahoma City, OK 73120
www.wn.org   1.800.242.6387

Children's Health Involving Parents

CHIP partners with parents in need to improve the health and well being of their children. By learning new skills and behaviors, parents become more confident, instilling good habits in their children.

CHIP of Greater Richmond, 222 W. Marshall St., Richmond, VA 23230
www.chipofrichmond.org   804.233.2850

Photographs

Beth Furgurson

Margaret Woodson Nea is a photographer, educator, and spiritual director with a strong personal connection with children. For twenty years she taught young children. She is the mother of two daughters and grandmother of five grandchildren. Her love of photographing has taken her from Kenya to Ecuador to Nepal to Thailand, to sixteen different countries. Her work has been exhibited in galleries and museums nationwide, including The United Nations, The International Photography Hall of Fame, The Museum of Southern History, The Museum of the Rockies, Princeton University, and The Children's Museum of Virginia. Her photographs have been published in her previous book, Children: Gifts of the Spirit, and in numerous other books, including Thomas Jefferson's Monticello and The Gardens of Monticello. She teaches photography, leads retreats, workshops, and conferences. She was named Artist-in-Residence at Episcopal High School in Alexandria and a visiting Artist at St. Catherine's School in Richmond. A Virginian, she is a graduate of Mary Baldwin College, holds a Master's Degree from the University of Richmond, and is a recent graduate of The Haden Institute.

Acknowledgments: my personal family, who loves and encourages me; my photographer friends, who teach and inspire me; the organizations that take me throughout the world; the children themselves whose eyes and spirit stay in my heart.